50 The Best Pizza Dishes in Town Recipes

By: Kelly Johnson

Table of Contents

- Margherita Pizza
- Pepperoni Pizza
- Quattro Formaggi (Four Cheese Pizza)
- Hawaiian Pizza
- BBQ Chicken Pizza
- Veggie Supreme Pizza
- Meat Lovers Pizza
- Margherita with Burrata
- White Pizza with Ricotta and Spinach
- Truffle Mushroom Pizza
- Prosciutto and Arugula Pizza
- Mediterranean Pizza with Feta and Olives
- Diavola Pizza (Spicy Italian Sausage)
- Neapolitan Pizza
- Pesto Chicken Pizza
- Buffalo Chicken Pizza
- Caprese Pizza
- Carbonara Pizza
- Fig and Goat Cheese Pizza
- Shrimp Scampi Pizza
- Smoked Salmon Pizza with Cream Cheese
- Spinach and Artichoke Pizza
- Sausage and Peppers Pizza
- Pear and Gorgonzola Pizza
- Roasted Veggie Pizza
- Anchovy Pizza
- BBQ Pulled Pork Pizza
- Meatball Pizza
- Salami and Mushroom Pizza
- Roasted Garlic and Kale Pizza
- Vegan Margherita Pizza
- Chicken Alfredo Pizza
- Sweet Potato and Bacon Pizza
- Breakfast Pizza with Eggs and Bacon
- Cacio e Pepe Pizza

- Cheeseburger Pizza
- Shrimp and Pesto Pizza
- Philly Cheesesteak Pizza
- Fig, Prosciutto, and Arugula Pizza
- Sausage and Onion Pizza
- Spicy Sausage and Ricotta Pizza
- Balsamic Glazed Chicken Pizza
- Mozzarella and Tomato Pizza
- Grilled Chicken and Veggie Pizza
- Caramelized Onion and Goat Cheese Pizza
- White Mushroom and Leek Pizza
- Apple and Bacon Pizza
- Eggplant Parmesan Pizza
- Spicy Tuna Pizza
- Truffle and Parmesan Pizza

Margherita Pizza

Ingredients:

- 1 pizza dough (store-bought or homemade)
- 1/2 cup tomato sauce
- 8 oz fresh mozzarella, sliced
- Fresh basil leaves
- Olive oil for drizzling

Instructions:

1. Preheat oven to 475°F (245°C).
2. Roll out the pizza dough and transfer to a baking sheet.
3. Spread tomato sauce over the dough, leaving a border for the crust.
4. Arrange mozzarella slices on top.
5. Bake for 10-12 minutes until the crust is golden and the cheese is bubbling.
6. Garnish with fresh basil and drizzle with olive oil before serving.

Pepperoni Pizza

Ingredients:

- 1 pizza dough
- 1/2 cup tomato sauce
- 8 oz mozzarella cheese, shredded
- 1/4 cup pepperoni slices
- Olive oil for drizzling

Instructions:

1. Preheat oven to 475°F (245°C).
2. Roll out pizza dough and place on a baking sheet.
3. Spread tomato sauce evenly over the dough.
4. Sprinkle with shredded mozzarella and arrange pepperoni slices on top.
5. Bake for 10-12 minutes or until the cheese is melted and the crust is crispy.
6. Drizzle with olive oil before serving.

Quattro Formaggi (Four Cheese Pizza)

Ingredients:

- 1 pizza dough
- 1/4 cup tomato sauce
- 2 oz mozzarella cheese
- 2 oz gorgonzola cheese
- 2 oz ricotta cheese
- 2 oz parmesan cheese, grated
- Fresh herbs for garnish

Instructions:

1. Preheat oven to 475°F (245°C).
2. Roll out pizza dough and spread a thin layer of tomato sauce.
3. Sprinkle mozzarella, gorgonzola, ricotta, and parmesan evenly over the dough.
4. Bake for 10-12 minutes until the cheese is melted and golden.
5. Garnish with fresh herbs and serve.

Hawaiian Pizza

Ingredients:

- 1 pizza dough
- 1/2 cup tomato sauce
- 8 oz mozzarella cheese, shredded
- 1/4 cup ham, diced
- 1/4 cup pineapple, diced
- Olive oil for drizzling

Instructions:

1. Preheat oven to 475°F (245°C).
2. Roll out the dough and spread tomato sauce over the base.
3. Top with mozzarella, diced ham, and pineapple.
4. Bake for 10-12 minutes or until the cheese is melted and the crust is golden.
5. Drizzle with olive oil before serving.

BBQ Chicken Pizza

Ingredients:

- 1 pizza dough
- 1/4 cup BBQ sauce
- 8 oz cooked chicken breast, shredded
- 8 oz mozzarella cheese, shredded
- 1/4 cup red onion, thinly sliced
- Fresh cilantro for garnish

Instructions:

1. Preheat oven to 475°F (245°C).
2. Roll out pizza dough and brush with BBQ sauce.
3. Layer shredded chicken, mozzarella, and red onion on top.
4. Bake for 10-12 minutes until the cheese is melted and the crust is golden.
5. Garnish with fresh cilantro and serve.

Veggie Supreme Pizza

Ingredients:

- 1 pizza dough
- 1/2 cup tomato sauce
- 8 oz mozzarella cheese, shredded
- 1/4 cup bell peppers, sliced
- 1/4 cup red onion, sliced
- 1/4 cup mushrooms, sliced
- 1/4 cup olives, pitted and sliced
- Fresh basil for garnish

Instructions:

1. Preheat oven to 475°F (245°C).
2. Roll out the pizza dough and spread tomato sauce on top.
3. Add mozzarella, bell peppers, red onion, mushrooms, and olives.
4. Bake for 10-12 minutes until the crust is golden and the cheese is melted.
5. Garnish with fresh basil before serving.

Meat Lovers Pizza

Ingredients:

- 1 pizza dough
- 1/2 cup tomato sauce
- 8 oz mozzarella cheese, shredded
- 1/4 cup pepperoni slices
- 1/4 cup sausage, cooked and crumbled
- 1/4 cup bacon, cooked and crumbled
- 1/4 cup ham, diced

Instructions:

1. Preheat oven to 475°F (245°C).
2. Roll out the pizza dough and spread tomato sauce evenly over it.
3. Top with mozzarella and meat toppings: pepperoni, sausage, bacon, and ham.
4. Bake for 10-12 minutes until cheese is melted and crust is golden.

Margherita with Burrata

Ingredients:

- 1 pizza dough
- 1/2 cup tomato sauce
- 8 oz fresh mozzarella
- 1 ball burrata cheese
- Fresh basil leaves
- Olive oil for drizzling

Instructions:

1. Preheat oven to 475°F (245°C).
2. Roll out the dough and spread tomato sauce over it.
3. Top with fresh mozzarella and bake for 10-12 minutes until the cheese melts.
4. Once the pizza is baked, add burrata and fresh basil.
5. Drizzle with olive oil before serving.

White Pizza with Ricotta and Spinach

Ingredients:

- 1 pizza dough
- 1/2 cup ricotta cheese
- 1 cup spinach, cooked and drained
- 8 oz mozzarella cheese, shredded
- Olive oil for drizzling

Instructions:

1. Preheat oven to 475°F (245°C).
2. Roll out the pizza dough and spread ricotta cheese as the base.
3. Add spinach and mozzarella cheese on top.
4. Bake for 10-12 minutes until golden and bubbly.
5. Drizzle with olive oil before serving.

Truffle Mushroom Pizza

Ingredients:

- 1 pizza dough
- 1/2 cup truffle oil
- 8 oz mixed mushrooms (such as cremini, shiitake, and oyster), sliced
- 8 oz mozzarella cheese, shredded
- 1/4 cup parmesan cheese, grated
- Fresh parsley for garnish

Instructions:

1. Preheat oven to 475°F (245°C).
2. Roll out the dough and brush with truffle oil.
3. Top with mozzarella, sliced mushrooms, and grated parmesan.
4. Bake for 10-12 minutes until the cheese is melted and golden.
5. Garnish with fresh parsley before serving.

Prosciutto and Arugula Pizza

Ingredients:

- 1 pizza dough
- 1/2 cup tomato sauce
- 8 oz mozzarella cheese, shredded
- 4 oz prosciutto slices
- 1 cup fresh arugula
- Olive oil for drizzling

Instructions:

1. Preheat oven to 475°F (245°C).
2. Roll out the dough and spread tomato sauce over it.
3. Add mozzarella and bake for 10-12 minutes until the cheese is melted and golden.
4. Once out of the oven, top with prosciutto and fresh arugula.
5. Drizzle with olive oil and serve.

Mediterranean Pizza with Feta and Olives

Ingredients:

- 1 pizza dough
- 1/2 cup tomato sauce
- 8 oz mozzarella cheese, shredded
- 1/4 cup feta cheese, crumbled
- 1/4 cup Kalamata olives, pitted and sliced
- 1/4 cup red onion, thinly sliced
- Fresh oregano for garnish

Instructions:

1. Preheat oven to 475°F (245°C).
2. Roll out the pizza dough and spread tomato sauce.
3. Top with mozzarella, feta, olives, and red onion.
4. Bake for 10-12 minutes until golden and bubbly.
5. Garnish with fresh oregano before serving.

Diavola Pizza (Spicy Italian Sausage)

Ingredients:

- 1 pizza dough
- 1/2 cup tomato sauce
- 8 oz mozzarella cheese, shredded
- 4 oz spicy Italian sausage, cooked and crumbled
- 1/4 cup red chili flakes
- Fresh basil for garnish

Instructions:

1. Preheat oven to 475°F (245°C).
2. Roll out pizza dough and spread tomato sauce evenly over it.
3. Add mozzarella and crumbled sausage.
4. Sprinkle with chili flakes and bake for 10-12 minutes until the cheese is golden.
5. Garnish with fresh basil and serve.

Neapolitan Pizza

Ingredients:

- 1 pizza dough
- 1/2 cup tomato sauce
- 8 oz fresh mozzarella cheese, sliced
- Fresh basil leaves
- Olive oil for drizzling

Instructions:

1. Preheat oven to 475°F (245°C).
2. Roll out the dough and spread a thin layer of tomato sauce.
3. Top with mozzarella and bake for 10-12 minutes until the crust is golden.
4. After baking, add fresh basil leaves and drizzle with olive oil.

Pesto Chicken Pizza

Ingredients:

- 1 pizza dough
- 1/4 cup pesto sauce
- 8 oz cooked chicken breast, shredded
- 8 oz mozzarella cheese, shredded
- 1/4 cup sun-dried tomatoes, sliced
- Fresh basil for garnish

Instructions:

1. Preheat oven to 475°F (245°C).
2. Roll out the dough and spread pesto sauce on top.
3. Add shredded chicken, mozzarella, and sun-dried tomatoes.
4. Bake for 10-12 minutes until cheese is melted and crust is golden.
5. Garnish with fresh basil before serving.

Buffalo Chicken Pizza

Ingredients:

- 1 pizza dough
- 1/4 cup buffalo sauce
- 8 oz cooked chicken breast, shredded
- 8 oz mozzarella cheese, shredded
- 1/4 cup blue cheese crumbles
- Celery leaves for garnish

Instructions:

1. Preheat oven to 475°F (245°C).
2. Roll out dough and spread buffalo sauce over it.
3. Add shredded chicken, mozzarella, and blue cheese crumbles.
4. Bake for 10-12 minutes until cheese is golden.
5. Garnish with celery leaves before serving.

Caprese Pizza

Ingredients:

- 1 pizza dough
- 1/2 cup tomato sauce
- 8 oz fresh mozzarella, sliced
- 1/4 cup cherry tomatoes, halved
- Fresh basil leaves
- Balsamic glaze for drizzling

Instructions:

1. Preheat oven to 475°F (245°C).
2. Roll out pizza dough and spread a thin layer of tomato sauce.
3. Add fresh mozzarella and cherry tomatoes.
4. Bake for 10-12 minutes until the cheese is melted and bubbly.
5. Garnish with fresh basil leaves and drizzle with balsamic glaze.

Carbonara Pizza

Ingredients:

- 1 pizza dough
- 1/2 cup alfredo sauce
- 8 oz mozzarella cheese, shredded
- 4 oz pancetta, diced
- 1/4 cup parmesan cheese, grated
- Fresh parsley for garnish

Instructions:

1. Preheat oven to 475°F (245°C).
2. Roll out pizza dough and spread a thin layer of alfredo sauce.
3. Top with mozzarella, pancetta, and parmesan cheese.
4. Bake for 10-12 minutes until the cheese is golden.
5. Garnish with fresh parsley before serving.

Fig and Goat Cheese Pizza

Ingredients:

- 1 pizza dough
- 1/2 cup olive oil
- 1/2 cup fig jam
- 8 oz goat cheese, crumbled
- 1/4 cup fresh rosemary, chopped
- 1/4 cup walnuts, chopped
- Fresh arugula for garnish

Instructions:

1. Preheat oven to 475°F (245°C).
2. Roll out the dough and brush with olive oil.
3. Spread a thin layer of fig jam over the dough.
4. Top with goat cheese, rosemary, and walnuts.
5. Bake for 10-12 minutes until the crust is golden and the cheese is melted.
6. Garnish with fresh arugula before serving.

Shrimp Scampi Pizza

Ingredients:

- 1 pizza dough
- 1/4 cup olive oil
- 2 garlic cloves, minced
- 1 lb shrimp, peeled and deveined
- 1/2 cup mozzarella cheese, shredded
- 1/4 cup parmesan cheese, grated
- Fresh parsley for garnish
- Zest of 1 lemon

Instructions:

1. Preheat oven to 475°F (245°C).
2. Roll out the dough and brush with olive oil.
3. Sauté garlic in olive oil over medium heat until fragrant, then add shrimp and cook until pink.
4. Arrange shrimp over the pizza dough and top with mozzarella and parmesan cheese.
5. Bake for 10-12 minutes until the cheese is golden and bubbly.
6. Garnish with fresh parsley and lemon zest before serving.

Smoked Salmon Pizza with Cream Cheese

Ingredients:

- 1 pizza dough
- 1/2 cup cream cheese, softened
- 1 tbsp fresh dill, chopped
- 4 oz smoked salmon, sliced
- 1/4 red onion, thinly sliced
- Capers for garnish
- Fresh lemon wedges

Instructions:

1. Preheat oven to 475°F (245°C).
2. Roll out the dough and spread a thin layer of cream cheese over it.
3. Top with smoked salmon, red onion, and a sprinkle of dill.
4. Bake for 8-10 minutes until the crust is golden.
5. Garnish with capers and serve with fresh lemon wedges.

Spinach and Artichoke Pizza

Ingredients:

- 1 pizza dough
- 1/2 cup alfredo sauce
- 1/2 cup spinach, sautéed
- 1/2 cup artichoke hearts, chopped
- 8 oz mozzarella cheese, shredded
- 1/4 cup parmesan cheese, grated

Instructions:

1. Preheat oven to 475°F (245°C).
2. Roll out the dough and spread alfredo sauce evenly over it.
3. Layer with sautéed spinach and artichoke hearts.
4. Top with mozzarella and parmesan cheese.
5. Bake for 10-12 minutes until golden and bubbly.

Sausage and Peppers Pizza

Ingredients:

- 1 pizza dough
- 1/2 cup tomato sauce
- 8 oz Italian sausage, cooked and crumbled
- 1 bell pepper, sliced
- 1/4 red onion, sliced
- 8 oz mozzarella cheese, shredded
- Fresh basil for garnish

Instructions:

1. Preheat oven to 475°F (245°C).
2. Roll out the dough and spread tomato sauce over it.
3. Add cooked sausage, bell pepper, and onion.
4. Top with mozzarella cheese.
5. Bake for 10-12 minutes until the cheese is melted and golden.
6. Garnish with fresh basil before serving.

Pear and Gorgonzola Pizza

Ingredients:

- 1 pizza dough
- 1/4 cup olive oil
- 1 pear, thinly sliced
- 4 oz gorgonzola cheese, crumbled
- 1/4 cup walnuts, chopped
- Fresh arugula for garnish

Instructions:

1. Preheat oven to 475°F (245°C).
2. Roll out the dough and brush with olive oil.
3. Layer the pear slices over the dough and sprinkle with gorgonzola cheese and walnuts.
4. Bake for 10-12 minutes until the crust is golden.
5. Garnish with fresh arugula before serving.

Roasted Veggie Pizza

Ingredients:

- 1 pizza dough
- 1/2 cup tomato sauce
- 1 zucchini, thinly sliced
- 1 bell pepper, sliced
- 1 red onion, sliced
- 1/2 cup mushrooms, sliced
- 8 oz mozzarella cheese, shredded
- Fresh basil for garnish

Instructions:

1. Preheat oven to 475°F (245°C).
2. Roll out the dough and spread a thin layer of tomato sauce.
3. Top with zucchini, bell pepper, onion, and mushrooms.
4. Add mozzarella cheese and bake for 10-12 minutes until golden.
5. Garnish with fresh basil before serving.

Anchovy Pizza

Ingredients:

- 1 pizza dough
- 1/2 cup tomato sauce
- 8 oz mozzarella cheese, shredded
- 8-10 anchovy fillets
- Fresh parsley for garnish

Instructions:

1. Preheat oven to 475°F (245°C).
2. Roll out the dough and spread tomato sauce evenly.
3. Add mozzarella cheese and top with anchovy fillets.
4. Bake for 10-12 minutes until the cheese is melted and golden.
5. Garnish with fresh parsley before serving.

BBQ Pulled Pork Pizza

Ingredients:

- 1 pizza dough
- 1/4 cup BBQ sauce
- 1 cup pulled pork
- 8 oz mozzarella cheese, shredded
- 1/4 red onion, thinly sliced
- Fresh cilantro for garnish

Instructions:

1. Preheat oven to 475°F (245°C).
2. Roll out the dough and spread BBQ sauce evenly.
3. Add pulled pork and mozzarella cheese.
4. Top with red onion slices and bake for 10-12 minutes.
5. Garnish with fresh cilantro before serving.

Meatball Pizza

Ingredients:

- 1 pizza dough
- 1/2 cup marinara sauce
- 6-8 small meatballs, crumbled or sliced
- 8 oz mozzarella cheese, shredded
- 1/4 cup parmesan cheese, grated
- Fresh basil for garnish

Instructions:

1. Preheat oven to 475°F (245°C).
2. Roll out the dough and spread marinara sauce evenly over it.
3. Add crumbled or sliced meatballs and top with mozzarella and parmesan cheese.
4. Bake for 10-12 minutes until golden and bubbly.
5. Garnish with fresh basil before serving.

Salami and Mushroom Pizza

Ingredients:

- 1 pizza dough
- 1/2 cup tomato sauce
- 8 oz salami, sliced
- 1/2 cup mushrooms, sliced
- 8 oz mozzarella cheese, shredded
- Fresh thyme for garnish

Instructions:

1. Preheat oven to 475°F (245°C).
2. Roll out the dough and spread tomato sauce evenly.
3. Add salami, mushrooms, and mozzarella cheese.
4. Bake for 10-12 minutes until the crust is golden and the cheese is bubbly.
5. Garnish with fresh thyme before serving.

Roasted Garlic and Kale Pizza

Ingredients:

- 1 pizza dough
- 1/4 cup olive oil
- 1 bulb garlic, roasted and mashed
- 2 cups kale, sautéed
- 8 oz mozzarella cheese, shredded
- Parmesan cheese, grated for garnish

Instructions:

1. Preheat oven to 475°F (245°C).
2. Roll out the dough and brush with olive oil.
3. Spread roasted garlic evenly over the dough.
4. Add sautéed kale and mozzarella cheese.
5. Bake for 10-12 minutes until golden.
6. Garnish with freshly grated parmesan before serving.

Vegan Margherita Pizza

Ingredients:

- 1 pizza dough
- 1/2 cup tomato sauce
- 1 cup vegan mozzarella cheese
- Fresh basil leaves
- Olive oil for drizzling

Instructions:

1. Preheat oven to 475°F (245°C).
2. Roll out the dough and spread a thin layer of tomato sauce over it.
3. Add vegan mozzarella cheese and bake for 10-12 minutes until the crust is golden and the cheese has melted.
4. Garnish with fresh basil leaves and drizzle with olive oil before serving.

Chicken Alfredo Pizza

Ingredients:

- 1 pizza dough
- 1/2 cup alfredo sauce
- 1 cup cooked chicken breast, shredded
- 8 oz mozzarella cheese, shredded
- Fresh parsley for garnish

Instructions:

1. Preheat oven to 475°F (245°C).
2. Roll out the dough and spread alfredo sauce evenly.
3. Top with shredded chicken and mozzarella cheese.
4. Bake for 10-12 minutes until golden and bubbly.
5. Garnish with fresh parsley before serving.

Sweet Potato and Bacon Pizza

Ingredients:

- 1 pizza dough
- 1/2 cup olive oil
- 1 sweet potato, thinly sliced and roasted
- 6 slices bacon, cooked and crumbled
- 8 oz mozzarella cheese, shredded
- Fresh rosemary for garnish

Instructions:

1. Preheat oven to 475°F (245°C).
2. Roll out the dough and brush with olive oil.
3. Layer with roasted sweet potato slices, bacon, and mozzarella cheese.
4. Bake for 10-12 minutes until golden and bubbly.
5. Garnish with fresh rosemary before serving.

Breakfast Pizza with Eggs and Bacon

Ingredients:

- 1 pizza dough
- 1/2 cup tomato sauce
- 4 eggs
- 6 slices bacon, cooked and crumbled
- 8 oz mozzarella cheese, shredded
- Fresh chives for garnish

Instructions:

1. Preheat oven to 475°F (245°C).
2. Roll out the dough and spread tomato sauce.
3. Add crumbled bacon and mozzarella cheese.
4. Make 4 small wells in the pizza, crack an egg into each, and bake for 10-12 minutes or until the eggs are set.
5. Garnish with fresh chives before serving.

Cacio e Pepe Pizza

Ingredients:

- 1 pizza dough
- 1/4 cup olive oil
- 1/2 cup pecorino romano cheese, grated
- 1/2 cup parmesan cheese, grated
- 1 tsp black pepper, freshly cracked

Instructions:

1. Preheat oven to 475°F (245°C).
2. Roll out the dough and brush with olive oil.
3. Sprinkle grated pecorino and parmesan cheese over the dough.
4. Add freshly cracked black pepper and bake for 10-12 minutes until golden and the cheese is melted.
5. Serve with a sprinkle of extra black pepper for added flavor.

Cheeseburger Pizza

Ingredients:

- 1 pizza dough
- 1/2 cup tomato sauce
- 1/2 lb ground beef, cooked and crumbled
- 8 oz cheddar cheese, shredded
- 1/4 red onion, thinly sliced
- Pickles, sliced
- Fresh lettuce for garnish

Instructions:

1. Preheat oven to 475°F (245°C).
2. Roll out the dough and spread a thin layer of tomato sauce.
3. Add crumbled cooked beef, cheddar cheese, and red onion slices.
4. Bake for 10-12 minutes until the crust is golden and the cheese is bubbly.
5. Garnish with fresh lettuce and pickles before serving.

Shrimp and Pesto Pizza

Ingredients:

- 1 pizza dough
- 1/2 cup pesto sauce
- 8-10 shrimp, cooked and peeled
- 8 oz mozzarella cheese, shredded
- Fresh basil for garnish

Instructions:

1. Preheat oven to 475°F (245°C).
2. Roll out the dough and spread pesto sauce evenly over the surface.
3. Top with cooked shrimp and mozzarella cheese.
4. Bake for 10-12 minutes until golden and bubbly.
5. Garnish with fresh basil leaves before serving.

Philly Cheesesteak Pizza

Ingredients:

- 1 pizza dough
- 1/2 cup provolone cheese, shredded
- 1/2 lb beef steak, thinly sliced
- 1/2 onion, sautéed
- 1/2 bell pepper, sautéed
- 1/4 cup mushrooms, sautéed
- Mozzarella cheese, shredded

Instructions:

1. Preheat oven to 475°F (245°C).
2. Roll out the dough and sprinkle with provolone cheese.
3. Layer thinly sliced beef, sautéed onion, bell pepper, and mushrooms over the cheese.
4. Add mozzarella cheese and bake for 10-12 minutes until golden.
5. Slice and serve hot, just like a classic Philly cheesesteak!

Fig, Prosciutto, and Arugula Pizza

Ingredients:

- 1 pizza dough
- 1/4 cup fig jam
- 8-10 slices prosciutto
- 1/2 cup mozzarella cheese, shredded
- 1/4 cup arugula leaves
- Balsamic glaze for drizzling

Instructions:

1. Preheat oven to 475°F (245°C).
2. Roll out the dough and spread a thin layer of fig jam.
3. Add prosciutto slices and mozzarella cheese.
4. Bake for 10-12 minutes until golden.
5. Remove from oven and top with fresh arugula and a drizzle of balsamic glaze.

Sausage and Onion Pizza

Ingredients:

- 1 pizza dough
- 1/2 cup marinara sauce
- 1/2 lb Italian sausage, crumbled
- 1/2 onion, thinly sliced
- 8 oz mozzarella cheese, shredded
- Fresh basil for garnish

Instructions:

1. Preheat oven to 475°F (245°C).
2. Roll out the dough and spread marinara sauce evenly over the surface.
3. Add crumbled sausage, onion slices, and mozzarella cheese.
4. Bake for 10-12 minutes until golden and bubbly.
5. Garnish with fresh basil leaves before serving.

Spicy Sausage and Ricotta Pizza

Ingredients:

- 1 pizza dough
- 1/2 cup marinara sauce
- 1/2 lb spicy Italian sausage, crumbled
- 8 oz ricotta cheese
- 8 oz mozzarella cheese, shredded
- Red pepper flakes for garnish

Instructions:

1. Preheat oven to 475°F (245°C).
2. Roll out the dough and spread marinara sauce.
3. Add crumbled sausage, ricotta cheese, and mozzarella cheese.
4. Sprinkle red pepper flakes for an extra kick.
5. Bake for 10-12 minutes until golden and bubbly.
6. Serve hot with more red pepper flakes if desired.

Balsamic Glazed Chicken Pizza

Ingredients:

- 1 pizza dough
- 1/2 cup balsamic glaze
- 1/2 cup cooked chicken breast, shredded
- 8 oz mozzarella cheese, shredded
- 1/4 cup red onion, thinly sliced
- Fresh basil leaves for garnish

Instructions:

1. Preheat oven to 475°F (245°C).
2. Roll out the dough and drizzle a thin layer of balsamic glaze.
3. Top with shredded chicken, mozzarella cheese, and red onion slices.
4. Bake for 10-12 minutes until golden and bubbly.
5. Garnish with fresh basil leaves before serving.

Mozzarella and Tomato Pizza

Ingredients:

- 1 pizza dough
- 1/2 cup marinara sauce
- 1 large tomato, thinly sliced
- 8 oz mozzarella cheese, sliced
- Fresh basil leaves for garnish
- Olive oil for drizzling

Instructions:

1. Preheat oven to 475°F (245°C).
2. Roll out the dough and spread marinara sauce.
3. Layer sliced tomatoes and mozzarella cheese over the sauce.
4. Bake for 10-12 minutes until the crust is golden and the cheese is bubbly.
5. Garnish with fresh basil leaves and drizzle with olive oil before serving.

Grilled Chicken and Veggie Pizza

Ingredients:

- 1 pizza dough
- 1/2 cup pesto sauce
- 1/2 cup grilled chicken breast, shredded
- 1/4 cup red bell pepper, thinly sliced
- 1/4 cup zucchini, thinly sliced
- 8 oz mozzarella cheese, shredded

Instructions:

1. Preheat oven to 475°F (245°C).
2. Roll out the dough and spread pesto sauce over it.
3. Add grilled chicken, red bell pepper, zucchini, and mozzarella cheese.
4. Bake for 10-12 minutes until golden and bubbly.
5. Slice and enjoy your fresh, grilled chicken and veggie pizza.

Caramelized Onion and Goat Cheese Pizza

Ingredients:

- 1 pre-made pizza crust or homemade dough
- 2 large onions, thinly sliced
- 2 tbsp olive oil
- 1 tbsp balsamic vinegar
- 1 cup goat cheese, crumbled
- 1 cup shredded mozzarella cheese
- Fresh thyme leaves
- Salt and pepper to taste

Instructions:

1. Preheat the oven to 475°F (245°C).
2. Heat olive oil in a skillet over medium heat. Add onions, season with salt, and cook, stirring occasionally, until golden brown (about 20-25 minutes). Add balsamic vinegar and cook for another 2-3 minutes.
3. Roll out the pizza dough onto a baking sheet or pizza stone.
4. Spread the caramelized onions evenly over the crust.
5. Sprinkle goat cheese and mozzarella over the onions.
6. Bake for 10-12 minutes or until the crust is golden and the cheese is melted.
7. Garnish with fresh thyme leaves before serving.

White Mushroom and Leek Pizza

Ingredients:

- 1 pre-made pizza crust or homemade dough
- 2 tbsp butter
- 1 large leek, thinly sliced (white and light green parts only)
- 2 cups sliced mushrooms (button or cremini)
- 1 cup shredded mozzarella cheese
- ½ cup grated Parmesan cheese
- 2 garlic cloves, minced
- Salt and pepper to taste

Instructions:

1. Preheat the oven to 475°F (245°C).
2. Melt butter in a skillet over medium heat. Add leeks and garlic, cooking for 5-7 minutes until softened. Add mushrooms and cook until golden, about 5 more minutes. Season with salt and pepper.
3. Roll out the pizza dough onto a baking sheet or pizza stone.
4. Spread the leek and mushroom mixture evenly over the crust.
5. Top with mozzarella and Parmesan cheese.
6. Bake for 10-12 minutes, or until the crust is golden and the cheese is bubbly.

Apple and Bacon Pizza

Ingredients:

- 1 pre-made pizza crust or homemade dough
- 2 medium apples, thinly sliced (Honeycrisp or Fuji recommended)
- 6 slices cooked bacon, crumbled
- 1 cup shredded mozzarella cheese
- ½ cup crumbled blue cheese (optional)
- 2 tbsp honey
- 1 tbsp olive oil
- 1 tsp fresh rosemary, chopped

Instructions:

1. Preheat the oven to 475°F (245°C).
2. Roll out the pizza dough onto a baking sheet or pizza stone. Brush with olive oil.
3. Arrange apple slices evenly over the crust. Sprinkle with bacon, mozzarella, and blue cheese (if using).
4. Drizzle honey over the toppings and sprinkle with rosemary.
5. Bake for 10-12 minutes, or until the crust is golden and the cheese is melted.

Eggplant Parmesan Pizza

Ingredients:

- 1 pre-made pizza crust or homemade dough
- 1 medium eggplant, sliced into thin rounds
- 1 cup marinara sauce
- 1 ½ cups shredded mozzarella cheese
- ½ cup grated Parmesan cheese
- 2 tbsp olive oil
- 1 tsp Italian seasoning
- Fresh basil for garnish

Instructions:

1. Preheat the oven to 475°F (245°C). Brush eggplant slices with olive oil and sprinkle with Italian seasoning. Roast on a baking sheet for 10-12 minutes until tender.
2. Roll out the pizza dough onto a baking sheet or pizza stone.
3. Spread marinara sauce evenly over the crust. Arrange roasted eggplant slices on top.
4. Sprinkle with mozzarella and Parmesan cheese.
5. Bake for 10-12 minutes, or until the crust is golden and the cheese is bubbly.
6. Garnish with fresh basil before serving.

Spicy Tuna Pizza

Ingredients:

- 1 pre-made pizza crust or homemade dough
- 1 can tuna, drained
- 1 cup marinara sauce
- 1 cup shredded mozzarella cheese
- ½ cup sliced red onions
- 1 tsp red chili flakes
- 1 tsp smoked paprika
- 1 tbsp olive oil
- Fresh parsley for garnish

Instructions:

1. Preheat the oven to 475°F (245°C).
2. Roll out the pizza dough onto a baking sheet or pizza stone.
3. Spread marinara sauce evenly over the crust.
4. Add tuna chunks and red onion slices. Sprinkle with mozzarella cheese, chili flakes, and smoked paprika.
5. Drizzle olive oil over the pizza.
6. Bake for 10-12 minutes, or until the crust is golden and the cheese is melted.
7. Garnish with fresh parsley before serving.

Truffle and Parmesan Pizza

Ingredients:

- 1 pre-made pizza crust or homemade dough
- 1 tbsp truffle oil
- 1 cup shredded mozzarella cheese
- ½ cup grated Parmesan cheese
- 1 cup arugula
- Salt and pepper to taste

Instructions:

1. Preheat the oven to 475°F (245°C).
2. Roll out the pizza dough onto a baking sheet or pizza stone.
3. Drizzle truffle oil over the crust. Sprinkle with mozzarella and Parmesan cheese.
4. Bake for 10-12 minutes, or until the crust is golden and the cheese is bubbly.
5. Top with fresh arugula, and season with salt and pepper before serving.

www.ingramcontent.com/pod-product-compliance
Lightning Source LLC
LaVergne TN
LVHW081505060526
838201LV00056BA/2951